An impartial account of the conduct of the excise towards the breweries in Scotland, particularly in Edinburgh; pointing out the beneficial effects of the new mode of survey, ...

ECCO
PRINT EDITIONS

Eighteenth Century
Collections Online
Print Editions

Gale ECCO Print Editions

Relive history with *Eighteenth Century Collections Online*, now available in print for the independent historian and collector. This series includes the most significant English-language and foreign-language works printed in Great Britain during the eighteenth century, and is organized in seven different subject areas including literature and language; medicine, science, and technology; and religion and philosophy. The collection also includes thousands of important works from the Americas.

The eighteenth century has been called "The Age of Enlightenment." It was a period of rapid advance in print culture and publishing, in world exploration, and in the rapid growth of science and technology – all of which had a profound impact on the political and cultural landscape. At the end of the century the American Revolution, French Revolution and Industrial Revolution, perhaps three of the most significant events in modern history, set in motion developments that eventually dominated world political, economic, and social life.

In a groundbreaking effort, Gale initiated a revolution of its own: digitization of epic proportions to preserve these invaluable works in the largest online archive of its kind. Contributions from major world libraries constitute over 175,000 original printed works. Scanned images of the actual pages, rather than transcriptions, recreate the works *as they first appeared.*

Now for the first time, these high-quality digital scans of original works are available via print-on-demand, making them readily accessible to libraries, students, independent scholars, and readers of all ages.

For our initial release we have created seven robust collections to form one the world's most comprehensive catalogs of 18th century works.

Initial Gale ECCO Print Editions collections include:

History and Geography
Rich in titles on English life and social history, this collection spans the world as it was known to eighteenth-century historians and explorers. Titles include a wealth of travel accounts and diaries, histories of nations from throughout the world, and maps and charts of a world that was still being discovered. Students of the War of American Independence will find fascinating accounts from the British side of conflict.

Social Science

Delve into what it was like to live during the eighteenth century by reading the first-hand accounts of everyday people, including city dwellers and farmers, businessmen and bankers, artisans and merchants, artists and their patrons, politicians and their constituents. Original texts make the American, French, and Industrial revolutions vividly contemporary.

Medicine, Science and Technology

Medical theory and practice of the 1700s developed rapidly, as is evidenced by the extensive collection, which includes descriptions of diseases, their conditions, and treatments. Books on science and technology, agriculture, military technology, natural philosophy, even cookbooks, are all contained here.

Literature and Language

Western literary study flows out of eighteenth-century works by Alexander Pope, Daniel Defoe, Henry Fielding, Frances Burney, Denis Diderot, Johann Gottfried Herder, Johann Wolfgang von Goethe, and others. Experience the birth of the modern novel, or compare the development of language using dictionaries and grammar discourses.

Religion and Philosophy

The Age of Enlightenment profoundly enriched religious and philosophical understanding and continues to influence present-day thinking. Works collected here include masterpieces by David Hume, Immanuel Kant, and Jean-Jacques Rousseau, as well as religious sermons and moral debates on the issues of the day, such as the slave trade. The Age of Reason saw conflict between Protestantism and Catholicism transformed into one between faith and logic -- a debate that continues in the twenty-first century.

Law and Reference

This collection reveals the history of English common law and Empire law in a vastly changing world of British expansion. Dominating the legal field is the *Commentaries of the Law of England* by Sir William Blackstone, which first appeared in 1765. Reference works such as almanacs and catalogues continue to educate us by revealing the day-to-day workings of society.

Fine Arts

The eighteenth-century fascination with Greek and Roman antiquity followed the systematic excavation of the ruins at Pompeii and Herculaneum in southern Italy; and after 1750 a neoclassical style dominated all artistic fields. The titles here trace developments in mostly English-language works on painting, sculpture, architecture, music, theater, and other disciplines. Instructional works on musical instruments, catalogs of art objects, comic operas, and more are also included.

The BiblioLife Network

This project was made possible in part by the BiblioLife Network (BLN), a project aimed at addressing some of the huge challenges facing book preservationists around the world. The BLN includes libraries, library networks, archives, subject matter experts, online communities and library service providers. We believe every book ever published should be available as a high-quality print reproduction; printed on-demand anywhere in the world. This insures the ongoing accessibility of the content and helps generate sustainable revenue for the libraries and organizations that work to preserve these important materials.

The following book is in the "public domain" and represents an authentic reproduction of the text as printed by the original publisher. While we have attempted to accurately maintain the integrity of the original work, there are sometimes problems with the original work or the micro-film from which the books were digitized. This can result in minor errors in reproduction. Possible imperfections include missing and blurred pages, poor pictures, markings and other reproduction issues beyond our control. Because this work is culturally important, we have made it available as part of our commitment to protecting, preserving, and promoting the world's literature.

GUIDE TO FOLD-OUTS MAPS and OVERSIZED IMAGES

The book you are reading was digitized from microfilm captured over the past thirty to forty years. Years after the creation of the original microfilm, the book was converted to digital files and made available in an online database.

In an online database, page images do not need to conform to the size restrictions found in a printed book. When converting these images back into a printed bound book, the page sizes are standardized in ways that maintain the detail of the original. For large images, such as fold-out maps, the original page image is split into two or more pages

Guidelines used to determine how to split the page image follows:

• Some images are split vertically; large images require vertical and horizontal splits.
• For horizontal splits, the content is split left to right.
• For vertical splits, the content is split from top to bottom.
• For both vertical and horizontal splits, the image is processed from top left to bottom right.

AN

IMPARTIAL ACCOUNT

OF THE

CONDUCT OF THE EXCISE

TOWARDS THE

BREWERIES IN SCOTLAND,

PARTICULARLY

IN EDINBURGH,

POINTING OUT

THE BENEFICIAL EFFECTS OF THE NEW MODE
OF SURVEY,

BY WHICH

Several THOUSAND POUNDS *per Annum* have been already
added to the Revenue in the EDINBURGH COLLECTION,

AND BY WHICH,

If generally adopted through *Scotland,* MANY THOUSANDS
more might be annually put into the EXCHEQUER,

NOT ONLY

WITHOUT DETRIMENT,

BUT WITH

ADVANTAGE TO THE MANUFACTURERS.

EDINBURGH:

PRINTED IN THE YEAR 1791.

INTRODUCTION.

IT is recorded as the faying of a very
great man*, that " an opinion of plenty
is one of the caufes of want;" and I believe
that in no cafe we can apply this expref-
fion more properly, than when fpeaking
of the liberty enjoyed by the people of
Britain. Puffed up by a confcioufnefs of
the excellence of the conftitution under
which we live, and intoxicated with the
idea that we are the moft free people
in the world, we tamely fubmit to fee
our conftitutional rights invaded, and
our liberties daily trampled upon, by a
fet of defigning and interefted men.

A　　　　　I MEAN

* Lord Bacon.

I MEAN not to go on in the ſtile of modern patriouſm, with a deſcant on the nature of liberty, the rights of mankind, &c.; the deſign of this treatiſe is to point out to the public the grievous, and indeed intolerable, oppreſſions under which a numerous, very uſeful, and important body of men, labour at preſent; and to ſhow, that through their oppreſſion, the community at large ſuſtains a very conſiderable injury.

IT is no doubt a matter of great difficulty for any individual, or even for any community, however reſpectable, to rid themſelves of an oppreſſion ſanctified by the name of law; or to make people in general believe that any others, beſides the oppreſſed parties themſelves, are at all intereſted in the matter; but it is an eſtabliſhed maxim, that an injury offered to any individual is a common cauſe, in which ſociety at large is intereſted; and,

in

in the prefent cafe, the intereft of every individual in Scotland is befides evidently engaged; fo that nothing farther than a mere ftatement of facts feems neceffary for the demonftration, and to awaken the attention, of the landholders of this country, to what fo nearly concerns them.

THAT it is the intereft of every perfon in this, as well as all other kingdoms, to drink wholefome and palatable liquor, rather than what has qualities of a different kind, cannot admit of a doubt *. As little can it be denied, that it is the in-

A 2

tereft

---

* It may appear fuperfluous to enlarge on the fuperiority of good malt liquor to bad, as this is evident to every one, but befides this, it is notorious, that when beer is made in fuch a way as to be unpleafant and unpalatable, other liquors are naturally fought after, and the pernicious cuftom of drinking fpirits to excefs is infenfibly introduced. In England, beer is the common beverage at every table, from the higheft nobility to the loweft mechanic. In that country it is a wholefome

tereft of every individual to have that liquor upon as reafonable terms as poffible; and thus the eafe and conveni-
ence of the brewer ought, in a reafonable
degree, to be confulted by every inhabi-
tant of Scotland. But befides this, there
are many other confiderations which re-
commend the brewers particularly to different claffes of the moft refpectable people in the kingdom. It is no matter,
fome will perhaps fay, whether we get
our

and agreeable liquor, and undoubtedly promotes
that hale vigour, and great ftrength of body, for
which the lower clafs of inhabitants there are remarkable. It is well known, that in England much
more work can be accomplifhed by labourers than
in Scotland. This muft be owing to the mode of
living; for a Scotfman who goes to England will
do more work there than in his own country. An
exceffive ufe of fpiritous liquors is undoubtedly one
caufe; and a very ftrong argument in favour of this
is, that wherever the practice becomes common a-
mong the labouring clafs of people, their mafters
foon find that much lefs work can be done by them
than formerly.

our beer from Scotland or England, provided we have it good and cheap. This argument indeed may go down with thofe who fancy themfelves unconnected with the reft of mankind, and is no doubt well calculated to anfwer the purpofes of an Englifh monopolift · but if we confider the vaft quantity of malt liquors ufed throughout Scotland, there is furely no perfon fo inconfiderate as not to perceive, that fending large fums of money to England, for a commodity which might be made to equal, nay, probably to greater advantage in our own, is a national lofs, and, of confequence, this practice merits the attention of every one, as well as that of the breweis themfelves. Now it is moft certain, that at prefent we are in danger of having this valuable branch of manufacture taken out of our hands, by reafon of the oppreffions under which the breweis in Scotland labour; and which are fo great, that no peifon poffef-

A 3   fed

fed of capital or fortune fufficient to carry on the bufinefs in a proper manner, feems inclined to engage in it, or probably will ever do fo, until matters be put on a footing fimilar to that on which they ftand in England.

EVERY one knows, that vaft quantities of malt liquors are continually imported from England, and proportional fums of money paid for them, which might be kept at home, if the manufacture was encouraged in fuch a manner among ourfelves as to enable the brewers to make their goods equal in quality to thofe of England, which could only be done by protecting them from the oppreffion of excifemen, and enforcing an equal mode of furvey. The Scots beer is undoubtedly inferior in quality to that of England; but why is it inferior? not furely for want of fkill or intelligence in the Scots manufacturers; for, in numberlefs inftances,

ftances, the Scots have fhewed themfelves at leaft equal to their fouthern neighbours in every fpecies of art or ingenuity. The truth is, that in Scotland the brewers who wifh to manufacture their liquors in a proper manner, and punctually to pay their duties, labour under oppreffions which are not known in England, and which it is the purport of this treatife to point out. Hence, not only porter is brought from London, but great quantities of beer are imported from Burton, Briftol, and even from Newcaftle. In the manufacture of this article, it is certain that the Englifh cannot boaft of the fmalleft fuperiority over us, provided we are put on an equality with them; and fuch fcandalous and expenfive importations are not only a lofs, but a *reproach* to this country, which muft very fenfibly be felt by every one who has the leaft fpirit, or regard for the nation in which he lives: for it is undoubtedly true,

to ufe the words of a celebrated writer
" That the profperity of the country is
the profperity of each citizen." The
lofs juft now mentioned is not the only
one arifing from the oppreffed ftate of the
Scots breweries. The confumpt of barley, one of the ftaple commodities of the
kingdom, is thereby materially affected.
It is the intereft of the landholder, therefore, to take this matter into his ferious
confideration ; and for the perufal of
the landed gentlemen, this treatife is particularly defigned. The intereft of the
farmer alfo coincides in this refpect with
that of the landholder. The diftillers
and brewers are well known to be the
principal confumers of the barley, and
the beft cuftomers the farmer has for
that article ; and it is now intended to
fhow, how, through a courfe of oppreffion,
by thofe who call themfelves executors
of the law, but in truth pervert it to their
own purpofes, the diftillers were ruined;
and,

and, by a continuation of the fame, the breweries, and other manufactures. fubject to the excife, are likely to experience a fimilar fate.

IT is well known that the manufacture of foap is now in a great meafure tranfferred from Scotland to England ; and that of ftarch has in many inftances been given up, merely from the arbitrary exactions of the excifemen, who thought themfelves intitled to demand a certain fum from the manufacturers, whether they made a proportionable quantity of goods or not. That this was really the cafe, cannot admit of a doubt; as a fpirited manufacturer, eminent in this branch of bufinefs, who had the courage to refift fuch impofition, was legally freed from the payment of no lefs than three thoufand pounds, with which the excife charged him, as duties on goods *never manufactured*.

It

IT is no doubt difficult, where any commodity is fubject to excife, to keep the manufacturer entirely free from inconvenience, in a confiftency with that watchfulnefs requifite for preventing frauds. In this refpect, the brewers may reafonably complain that the laws are exceffively fevere; but even this feverity is nothing to the *illegal* and *partial* oppreffion exercifed by the fubordinate agents of excife. There is not the leaft doubt, that where a tax is laid upon any fpecies of manufacture, fome will always be found willing to evade the payment by every poffible method. But it is equally certain, that where the tax-gatherers are allowed any difcretionary power, they will be as willing to *opprefs*, as the manufacturer is to *fmuggle*; and this the more readily, as the collectors of taxes are fometimes chofen from a clafs of men by no means celebrated either for civility, ty, good manners, or adequate ideas of juftice.

On the whole, it is intended by the prefent performance, to prove, from un-doubted facts, that all defcriptions of ex-cife-men have plainly fhewed, that their intention was not to encreafe the revenue, but, for their own intereft, to allow the brewers what liberties they pleafed, and not to check them in defrauding it ; that in this they have been countenanced by thofe who are appointed to enforce the execution of the excife laws ; and, I am forry to add, that thofe who are appointed and ought to be *judges* of the law, have not found fault with their conduct, even when detected in the moft fcandalous inftances of oppreffion and injuftice. The confequence of all this hath been, the diminution of the revenue, the def-truction of individuals, and the ruin-ing of a moft ufeful branch of manufacture,

facture, which many have abandoned, merely on account of the vexations they daily met with, and from which they could neither perceive nor hope for any relief. This muſt be looked upon as a great misfortune, when we conſider, that Scotland, by reaſon of its ſituation, the cheapneſs of labour, and the favourable climate it enjoys for fermentation, is particularly well adapted for the manufacture of malt liquors. Were this buſineſs properly carried on, and advantage taken of theſe favourable circumſtances juſt mentioned, there is not the leaſt doubt, that this country might not only manufacture as much malt liquor as ſuffices for its own conſumpt, but export vaſt quantities to foreign parts. This has indeed been attempted, and it has been found, that beer of a good quality would be a valuable article of commerce, not only on the Eaſtern continent, but in the Weſt Indies alſo; though all

ſchemes

fchemes of carrying on a trade of this kind have hitherto failed, and muft fail, unlefs the obftacles which hitherto have ftood in the way, from the oppreffive mode of collecting the revenue, be removed. The attention of the landed gentlemen, therefore, and of the Chamber of Commerce, who have already regulated feveral branches of bufinefs in this country, is requefted. It is only by the unanimity and ftrenuous efforts of the community at large, that redrefs from any public grievance can be obtained; and in the prefent cafe, it is hoped that every one will confider himfelf as particularly interefted, fo that all ranks may unite in their endeavours for the removal of evils of fuch enormous magnitude.

CASE

OF THE

SCOTS BREWERY;

ALSO OF THE

DISTILLERY PRIOR TO THE LICENSE.

BEFORE we enter into any particulars refpecting the prefent ftate of thefe manufactures, it will be neceffary to eradicate an idea, which, however common, is certainly very far from being founded in fact, viz. That neither of thefe branches of bufinefs can be carried on without fmuggling. The reafon of this notion is, that people, unacquainted with the bufinefs, fuppofe the produce, both of worts and fpirits, from a certain quantity of grain, to be fo fmall, that the manufacturer cannot from thence afford to pay the duty. Hence it is commonly fuppofed, that the only

emoluments

emoluments enjoyed either by brewers or diftillers, arife from the quantities of liquor they can fecret from the excifemen; and in this view, both branches would not only be ultimately fraudulent, but fo precarious and uncertain, that no perfon could be thought willing to engage in them. The truth, however, is, that in thefe branches of bufinefs, as well as in every other department of life, people will always find the proverb verified, that *honefty is the beft policy*; and the brewer or diftiller, who pays his duties without any attempt to fmuggle, will be a more confiderable gainer in the end, than he who evades them in every poffible way. The extenfive manner in which the brewing bufinefs is carried on in almoft every town in England, will ferve to fubftantiate this fact.

THERE are, it muft be owned, fome perfons who will always attempt to evade a duty, however flight, and imagine that they confult their own intereft when they do fo. No doubt this would be found a profitable method of carrying on bufinefs, could they evade the duties, and at the fame time have

every

every other advantage they can propofe to themfelves by paying them, but this is far from being the cafe. Brewing of malt liquors is an art of a very complicated nature; its proceffes are delicate, and the criterions which diftinguifh the completion of its various operations require to be accurately inveftigated; fo that to make malt liquor in perfection is perhaps more difficult than any domeftic art we have. The preliminary part of the procefs, *viz.* mafhing and taking off the liquor, requires a great exertion of fkill on the part of the brewer. It is by no means eafy to extract the ftrength of the malt to the utmoft advantage, and give the wort the greateft perfection of which it is capable. In this operation the variation of a few degrees of heat will make a very perceptible change, both as to ftrength and other properties. Even in the fimple operation of boiling, the ftricteft attention is requifite; as the copper often receives a good extract from the malt, and gives back a bad wort. Fermentation, the principal procefs, is at once the moft difficult to conduct, the moft liable to error, and the moft important to the intereft of the

B   brewer.

brewer. The prefervative quality of the beer, its diftinguifhing flavour, its body, and fprituofity, all depend, for their very exiftence, on the judicious management of this operation.

FROM this account of the nature of brewing, it is eafy to fee how pernicious the practice of fmuggling muft be, and how detrimental in every refpect to the quality of the liquor. How is it poffible for a fmuggler to manufacture his goods in a proper manner, when obliged to beftow, in defrauding the revenue, one-half, or the greater part of that attention, which his bufinefs ought folely to engrofs ? How can good beer be made, when the liquor is perpetually difturbed in its fermentation ; when not properly boiled ; when obliged to remain till it is too cold, or perhaps ufed too hot; or when its qualities are injured by noxious air in the hiding-places to which fmugglers are obliged to carry it ? The deficiencies hence arifing muft be deducted, in the firft place, from the profits of the fmuggler ; and in many cafes even this will be fufficient to overbalance what he makes by evading

the

the duty. But, befides this, there are other particulars which muft be taken into confideration. The utmoft activity on the part of the manufacturer cannot always elude the vigilance of the excifeman. If he happens to be a man of integrity, many quantities of liquor will unavoidably be detected, and the penalties, when laid on with a view to fupprefs fmuggling, confequent upon this detection, muft diminifh the profits ftill more ; add to all which, that a great part of the brewer's time muft be taken up in attending and courting the excife-man, keeping him out of the way, and attempting to procure his favour. He muft fubject himfelf to perfons remarkable neither for their refinement of manners, nor the liberality of their fentiments nay, if he happens to have to do with more than one at a time, perhaps the utmoft impartiality in diftributing his favours may not be able to fecure him from the threats of abfolute ruin. [*]

B 2

IT

[*] Of this fome very laughable inftances might be given.—An affiftant officer was appointed by Mr Maitland, the late furveyor-general, to watch a brewer's copper, and that he might keep watch in the moft *proper* manner, he was promifed by the brewer a pair of elegant

IT will now be proper to confider the detriment arifing to the brewers from the behaviour of the excife-men themfelves. As we cannot fuppofe all the brewers in Scotland to be vicious, neither can we reafonably fuppofe all the excife-men to be virtuous The end propofed by government in laying on duties, is to produce a revenue for its own purpofes; that

piftols, and had a good dinner into the bargain. The gauger fhewed his zeal for the revenue, by defiring the brewer's fervants not to carry away *all* the liquor till he returned from dinner, and till this was ready, he looked over the window, that if any of his brethren happened to come in the way, he might acquaint them that their prefence was entirely unneceffary. For fome unknown reafon there was a delay made on the brewer's part in giving the promifed reward. The gauger not receiving the piftols as he expected, refolved to let the brewer know that excife-officers were not to be trifled with. He therefore took the firft opportunity of detecting a concealed barrel of beer, which ought to have paid *elevenpence* of duty. Information of the feizure was given, and the brewer was fined L. 7 Sterling. Such men there are, no doubt, in every department but we are forry to conclude this anecdote, with informing the public, that though the commiffioners ordered an enquiry into the affair, and the above facts were fubftantiated by the depofitions of witneffes, the offender, inftead of being punifhed for his infamous conduct, was foon after promoted to be a fett'd

that of the excife-men may reafonably be
thought to make money to themfelves. This
cannot be done where the brewers take care
to pay their duties exactly; for the excife-officers have no fhare in the revenues, tho' they
are entitled to a fhare in the fines, where any
fraudulent practice is difcovered on the part
of the manufacturer. They have therefore
an inducement to prefer the fmuggler to the
fair trader ; and though now and then difco-
veries muft be made, in order to make the
commiffioners believe that they are active and
diligent officers, as well as for other reafons;
(for if no detections were made, the excife-
men could avowedly have nothing but their
bare falary), yet it may reafonably be fuppofed, that much fmuggling has been practifed,

without

officer, and afterwards obtained the charge of the New
Glafs-houfe at Leith, with an increafe of falary   Other inftances might be authenticated, where brewers or diftillers
have been reduced to a very embarraffing fituation, by giving
one excife-man only boiled beef, while another in a diftant
quarter had roaft, in which cafe the boiled-beef-officer never
failed to threaten vengeance on the manufacturer, which
could only be avoided by giving him next day roaft beef,
with the addition of plumb-pudding, by way of making
amends.

without any exertion made on the part of the excise-men to prevent it, and that some way or other, they find it not disadvantageous to their own interest to allow the brewers to take such liberties. Hence it is in the power of an excise-officer to ruin even a fair trader, by allowing one of his brethren to smuggle to such a degree that he can reduce the price of his goods below what they can be fairly sold at*; and there is no doubt, that thus, not only individuals have been hurt, but the public at large considerably injured, by having liquors of a bad quality imposed upon them. From this cause particularly we may derive that vast importation of malt liquors from England, the value of which is supposed to be little, if any thing, under L. 200,000 *per annum;* and of this it is computed that the city of Edinburgh alone imports to the amount of L.40,000.

WHILE

---

* A demonstration of the truth of this assertion is, that some years ago, spirits were frequently sold below the value of the duty imposed upon them by government how then was it possible for the fair trader to keep his ground against such rivals?

WHILE the excife-men have it thus in their power to opprefs the fair trader, there is no doubt that they will frequently exercife it, as they derive no advantage from them, though they do from the fmugglers. Unhappily the great liberties allowed them by the late acts of parliament, furnifh many opportunities of oppreffion, which they had not before. They are now empowered to go into the houfe of any perfon who deals in excifeable commodities, and to remain there at any time of the day or night, as long as they pleafe. It is eafy to fee that this power, when lodged in improper hands, may foon become intolerable to thofe upon whom it is excercifed, and it is not long fince the gate of an eminent brewer in Edinburgh was broken down by a troop of excife-men, and he himfelf fined in five pounds, on pretence of admittance not being readily granted, though it was then between twelve and one at night, and immediate admittance could not be expected. The particular circumftances attending this tranfaction, every one of which can be well authenticated, will ferve to point out its enormity. The trader had been that day brewing, the

excife-

excife-officers had watched him till feven at night, had feen the extent of his operations, all of them finifhed, and his fervants gone home. There was a natural impoffibility that the operation could be refumed that night, with the fmalleft hopes of fuccefs, or that the revenue could, in any manner of way, be defrauded in four or five hours. He might have indeed mafhed another quantity, but no human power could have run off the worts, and boiled them in the time; fo that next day's furvey would certainly have detected him. The furvey at midnight, therefore, was *evidently* made, *not with a view to prevent the revenue from being defrauded*, but to diftrefs and put the brewer to inconvenience. The inftructions given to excife-officers how to behave in thefe nocturnal furveys, enjoin a quite different mode of procedure. Inftead of obeying the orders of their fuperiors, however, the excife-men, in the prefent cafe, behaved as already related; but even this was lefs culpable than the partiality we have now to relate.—Another brewer, exactly in the predicament of the former one, was that very night furveyed, and his gate

in

in like manner broken open, both which out-
rages were contrary to law, the former was
profecuted, and fined for non-admittance, but
no profecution was commenced againft the
other. How can the folicitor or furveyor account for fuch evident partiality? It is the
boaft of *Englifhmen*, that " the leaft confiderable man among them has an intereft equal to
the proudeft nobleman, in the laws and conftitution of the country," but in Scotland it
feems to be otherwife. Here a pitiful defpot
of an excife-man or folicitor, can fufpend the
execution of the laws, and, like a fovereign,
grant pardons at pleafure; and that even tho'
bound in duty, and by oath of office, to act in
a different manner.

It is difficult to imagine the lengths in effrontery to which men will go when once they
have thrown off the fhackles of virtue, and
have little fear of the reftraints of law. I
have been informed, upon the authority of
the excife-men themfelves, that in feveral
towns in this country, it has been for fome
time cuftomary, that brewers fhould be fined
at certain intervals, and at fuch a rate as
would

would augment the falary of the excife-offi-cers L. 20 annually, and this whether the former have been detected in any offence or not. It is impoffible to look upon this prac-tice in any other light than as an agreement, on the part of the excife-men, to tolerate fmug-gling for a certain fum paid to themfelves. This, however, is not the worft; the fines are not only arbitrarily laid on, but exacted with the higheft degree of partiality. Inftances can be produced, where brewers, detected in frauds to a confiderable amount, have been allowed to efcape on paying only 2 and a-half *per cent.* of the legal penalty, while from others, 50, 60, 70 or 80 *per cent,* and even full penal-ties, have been exacted. Practices of this kind have the moft mifchievous tendency. The brewers who are thus favoured have an encouragement to continue the practice of fmuggling; they run themfelves into all the inconveniencies attending this practice ; make liquors of a bad quality, and endeavour to un-derfell their neighbours. This method of underfelling is not only a great detriment to the trade in general, and may frequently be the ruin of individuals, but is difadvantage-

ous

ous to the public at large ; and for this plain reafon, that, whenever fuch kind of rivalfhip commences, a great quantity of goods, improperly manufactured, are fure to be brought to market.

In taking a general view of the whole bufinefs refpecting both the diftillery and brewery in Scotland, it muft certainly appear very ftrange, that the excife-officers fhould always have appeared willing to direct their vengeance, in a particular manner, againft the fair trader, rather than the fraudulent dealer. A few years ago, the London diftillers raifed a clamour that they were underfold by thofe in Scotland. The excife joined in the cry, and every fevere and unjuftifiable ftretch of power was made ufe of to ruin that branch of manufacture   It was not fufficient to put in execution the laws, as they ftood at that time, with the greateft rigour The hydrometer, an inftrument never before ufed in making furveys, was introduced ; and that not by the legiflature, but by the excife. The law fuppofed a certain proportion of fpirits to be produced from the *wafh*, or liquor in its raw ftate,

and

and the duties were to be regulated according to this quantity. If the manufacturer could, by any improvement in the operation, produce a greater quantity of fpirits, the furplus was naturally fuppofed to belong to himfelf; but even this advantage, which no perfon of common fenfe would have refufed, was denied by the zealous officers of excife. If the diftiller produced more than the legal quantity, he was fuppofed to have done it from concealed wafh; if he produced lefs, he was ftill liable to the duty in its full amount. From fuch fcandalous behaviour we may juftly infer, that the ruin of the manufacturer, not the increafe of revenue, was at that time the object of excife-men; and their conduct from that time to the prefent has abundantly verified the affertion. In every inftance their power was ftretched to the utmoft; and in every inftance the oppreffion of the excife far exceeded the intention of the law, while that oppreffion was executed with fuch an high hand, and with fuch infolence, as was altogether intolerable. By the ftatute at that time a diftiller's ftock was to be furveyed at leaft once in thirty days, and the excife-officers

were

were allowed to enter the works of the manufacturers in the night. In confequence of
this permiffion, the diftilleries were infefted
with excife-men day and night, doors were
forced open, and walls beat down, if inftanta-
neous admiffion was not given; as if locks
and bolts fhould have been diffolved in a moment, by the powerful magic of their breath.
Every thing that could poffibly be done to
lay the trader under difadvantages, was done,
as if his ruin had been to enrich the whole
Board of Excife.

Happily for the diftillers, they have now
got free from fuch intolerable oppreffion, and,
by paying the duties on the contents of the
ftill, are enabled to carry on their works with
profit to themfelves, and advantage to the
country. With the brewers it is otherwife,
and they ftill groan under the iron hand of
oppreffion. The difficulties under which
they laboured were indeed fo great, that the
bufinefs was in danger of being totally loft,
by reafon of the inferior quality of the liquors
produced, and which left a decided fuperiority in favour of the Englifh manufacturer.
The

The commencement of the new diſtillery-act, while it gave relief to the manufacturers of ſpirits, ſeemed only to render the caſe of the brewers more deſperate. The exciſe redoubled their oppreſſions; and they ſeemed now to have adopted a plan of ſqueezing from the brewers, thoſe emoluments which had formerly been derived from the diſtillery, but which, by the new act, were irrecoverably gone. The firſt ſtep to accompliſh this purpoſe, was to be remiſs in ſurveying, that every one who choſe to ſmuggle might have an opportunity of doing ſo. Thus indeed the revenue would not be increaſed, but as frequent detections could not be avoided, the exciſe-officers, who reaped the benefit of theſe, would be able to put ſome money in their pockets. Along with this laxity of ſurvey, great lenity was ſhewn by the ſolicitor of exciſe in the juſtice of peace courts, by prevailing on the judges to accommodate the proportion of fines to be paid, to the wiſhes of the traders themſelves. Thus the whole buſineſs was put upon the worſt footing imaginable. The aim of the manufacturer now was not to make his liquors as good as poſſible, but to

ſmuggle

fmuggle as much as he could with impunity, and to underfell his neighbours. Hence a very confiderable reduction in the price of malt liquors took place, fo that ftrong ale in Edinburgh was brought down from 48 to 33 fhillings *per* hogfhead. In this, however, it is certain that neither the brewers nor the public were much obliged to thofe who had thus lowered the price, the former being obliged to manufacture their goods in an improper manner, with very uncertain profit; and the latter being fupplied with liquors of fuch bad quality, that they could fcarce be ufed, and for which the lownefs of the price was no compenfation.

But, befides the confequences juft now mentioned, another event, of great importance to both parties, had now taken place; *viz.* that all the manufacturers were in the power of the excife the fcheme was accomplifhed, and it was time for thofe who were to reap the benefit of it to begin their exactions. Inftead of the lenity which had fo lately been fhewn, the utmoft feverity was ufed. The moft unequal methods of furvey took place, and, though numberlefs opportunities were ftill given to evade the duties, yet this, as might eafily be feen, was only to accumulate the number of fines; for as to the revenue, it did not rife, notwithftanding the feverity, or rather oppreffion made ufe of. With regard to the payment of the fines, which were now very numerous, the moft fhameful partiality was ufed. The delinquents, as ufual, were profecuted before the Juftices, or King's Court *, as it is called. Some manufacturers, known

---

* From the title which this court bears, and the importance of the caufes frequently brought before it, the reader will naturally fuppofe that the judges are felected from among the moft intelligent and independent gentlemen in the county So far, however, is this from being the cafe, that even the *exiftence* of fuch a court has been doubted by fome of them, when queftions were put concerning its tranfactions As the matter is managed at prefent, the court has the appearance of being calculated rather to put money in the pockets of the folicitor of excife, and fome other friends, than deciding impartially on the caufes brought before it. It is notorious, that only two or three gentlemen commonly attend as judges, and it cannot but be matter of furprife to many, why thefe gentlemen fhould conftantly take the trouble upon them, efpecially as one of them is a juftice only *ex officio*, and at prefent a Baron of the Exchequer Ill-natured

known to be friends to the Excife, were either acquitted altogether, or fined in very trifling fums. others, whofe crimes feemed to be no greater, were very highly affeffed; and this the more efpecially if they had the boldnefs to make any defence; nay, it is even faid that threats of imprifonment were ufed, if they prefumed to perfift in afferting their innocence; and, to add to this oppreffion, the folicitor had

C frequently

people would fay, that they derive *fome emolument* from their attendance, and it cannot be fuppofed that their dining with the excife-men after the meetings can add greatly to their refpectability It is abfolutely unknown how or when the judges are fummoned, and feveral gentlemen of very independent fortunes have expreffed an inclination to attend, if they only knew the time and place where the meetings are held The fines exacted from the delinquents are divided equally between the folicitor of excife, the clerk of the court, the excifeman, and the king It is evidently, therefore, the intereft of the folicitor and clerk to have as many people fined as poffible, and the former conftantly affumes, as much as in his power, the authority of a judge himfelf, and it is juftly to be regretted, that no inquiry has ever been made into his tranfactions in this refpect. It is undoubtedly worth the attention of fuch a numerous and refpectable body as the Juftices of Mid-Lothian, to regulate the proceedings of a court which bears their name, and where they have all a right to fit as judges, in fuch a manner as that they may correfpond with the dignity of character univerfally attributed to the gentlemen of that county.

frequently the infolence to ridicule, brow-beat, and infult thofe who ftood on their defence. Nay, fo great was the opinion this gentleman entertained of his own oratory, that he frequently attempted to perfuade the court that his integrity was fo great, that he would bring no perfon before them who was not guilty! Befides this, fuch mean tricks and chicanery were frequently put in practice, as would have difgraced the loweft of the pettifogging tribe; fuch as protracting the caufes from one diet to another; by which decreets in abfence might be obtained; and even appointing an hour when the party was to be heard in his defence, while, prior to the hour agreed upon, a decreet againft him was awarded. Still, however, the revenue was not increafed; for it is certainly a juft obfervation, that fmuggling cannot be fuppreffed by feverity and oppreffion; as the traders muft naturally look upon fuch conduct in the Excife as a fufficient excufe for any thing they can do to evade the duty. In the prefent cafe, indeed, there feemed to be no intention to augment the revenue, but a vile fcheme to induce the traders to fmuggle, and thus at once to defraud the revenue, en-

flave

slave and impoverish themselves, and supply the public with bad liquors, on purpose to enrich the solicitor and excise-man.

In such a state of confusion, it is easily to see that the only chance which any trader had to preserve himself from ruin, was by smuggling as much as possible. The prices were much reduced, so that the duties could not be paid, strong ale being brought down from 48 to 33 Shillings *per* hogshead, as already mentioned, porter was also reduced from two guineas to 30 Shillings *per* hogshead, and what was worse, there seemed to be no possibility of finding a remedy; for as the favourites of Excise had every opportunity of evading the duty at very little expence, the rest of the manufacturers were obliged to follow their example; and thus the subjection of the whole trade to the Excise seemed to be complete and irremediable. Private meetings now began to be held among the brewers, to consider of some method of saving themselves from ruin, and thus some general resolutions were gradually formed, which, it is hoped, may in time produce the most salutary effects.

Their

Their eyes were now thoroughly opened to their own interest, and they perceived, that while the practice of smuggling was continued, they could neither supply their customers with liquors of a proper quality, nor make a reasonable profit for themselves. The only method of relieving themselves from the oppression under which they laboured, was evidently a full and voluntary payment of the duties to government. Indeed, matters were now come to such a crisis, that without adopting this method, there seemed no possibility of preventing the whole trade from being transferred to England. Not only porter and strong ale were imported from that country, in great quantities, but some had even begun to import small beer also. The only persons who had gained by the smuggling scheme, were the solicitor, the excise-officers, and others connected with them, among whom the fines were divided. The public, by having liquor at a cheaper rate, seemed to share some of the profits ; but this was greatly overbalanced by its bad quality. That the zeal of the officers of excise at that time was not directed to the advancement of the

revenue,

revenue, but to the detection of *some part* of the frauds which they allowed the manufacturers to commit, is evident from the following anecdote. Mr Bonnar, present solicitor of excise, was well known to have frequent meetings with Maitland, the general surveyor, and other supervisors. At these meetings, the question was not how to secure the revenue from frauds, but how to detect them, and to determine whose traders paid most fines; never seeming to imagine that the whole duties were paid, or that it was their own business to cause them be paid. Mr Bonnar, who, (like the devil in a club of witches) always presided in these assemblies, commended his inferior agents in proportion to the dexterity they had shewed in the detection of frauds, and did not scruple to rebuke very sharply those who seemed to be negligent in this respect; threatening them with a total loss of his favour, if they did not bring him in those fines. In particular, he charged Mr Aberdeen, an active and diligent officer, with having brought him in no frauds for some time past. The latter, probably conscious of having discharged his duty in an honest and

faithful

faithful manner, retorted feverely upon Bonnar; telling him, that the traders under his
jurifdiction paid their duties very well; that
he could not act fuch a villainous part as to
allow frauds to be made to the detriment of
the revenue; and that he had more right
to find fault with Bonnar himfelf, who had
not profecuted frauds, to the great detriment
of the revenue, which he had difcovered, and
that he had got no account whatever of feveral
which had been ordered to him for profecution; that allowing frauds to be committed in any inftance, was mifleading other traders into a notion that they might follow the
feme practice with impunity, &c. On this
Bonnar was highly offended; told Aberdeen
that he would do for him; a violent uproar
enfued; the meeting broke up in confufion;
and Aberdeen fuffered for his prefump-
tion, by being foon after removed to Kil-
marnock. From that time forward, neither
fupervifors nor other officers had the courage to oppofe Mr Bonnar or Mr Maitland,
in any thing they thought proper to fay; nay,
they were even afraid to afk for the fhares
of fines to which they were juftly entitled,
leaft Bonnar or Maitland fhould take offence.

The

The fame inattention to the real duty of an excife-officer was evident from the behaviour of Mr Maitland, who, by a report he gave into the Board of Excife, had intereft to get Peter Torbet, a moft active and diligent officer, feverely reprimanded, becaufe for two months he had difcovered no frauds; without confidering that he had really doubled the duty of excife in his divifion, during the time he refided there. It is furprifing that it fhould be imagined that the duty of a gauger is only to *detect* frauds, without attempting to prevent them; and it is equally furprifing for any perfon to fuppofe, that if frauds are *prevented*, there fhould remain as many as before to be detected.

WHILE the brewers had fuch men to deal with, it is evident that there was but little profpect of their being able to better themfelves; as thofe, to whom they were at that time in fubjection, could eafily overturn their fchemes of reformation, by allowing fome of their brethren to efcape with impunity; who, continuing to fell at their reduced prices, would render it impracticable for the reft to carry on their trade with profit, if they paid the

duty

duty. Thus they were obliged to folicit from the Board of Excife, an alteration in the mode of furvey, by which it fhould be rendered as difficult as poffible for the manufactu er to conceal from the excife-officers any quantity of liquor worth while; and with this view they prefented to the Board certain propofi-tions, by which the conduct of the gaugers fhould in future be regulated.

THESE being confidered by their Honours, met with approbation; and the new mode of furvey was put in execution. The good ef-fects of this change were inftantly perceived, by the vaft increafe of revenue; which, from L. 300, or little more, arofe to very near L. 1000 *per* month, as will fully appear from the fol-lowing comparative ftatement of the duties for fome years paft :———

		L.	s.	d	
Years ending Midfummer	1785	4274	9	9	Mr Maitland Surveyor Ge-neral
	1786	4370	5	0	
	1787	4825	7	2	
	1788	4691	15	8	
	1789	8011	15	11	Mr Burnet Sur-veyor General.
	1790	10,817	12	9	

A RISE

A RISE in the revenue even took place for two months before the new mode of furvey was adopted, but this was entirely owing to the alarm raifed amongft the excifemen, and to the time taken up by the Honourable Board, in deliberating on the propriety of accepting the propofals. A Committee had been appointed in November 1788, for putting in execution the propofed plan, but owing to the delay juft mentioned, though the propofals were dated on the 8th of that month, they were not adopted by the Board till January 5th 1789. The principal caufe of this very fudden rife in the revenue, was the ufe of an inftrument propofed by the Committee, called a *Granometer*, which, by meafuring the quantity of grain ufed, at any time of the operation, could at once fhew the precife number of bolls mafhed, in whatever ftate they are found, whether wet or dry. Thus, the number of barrels, whether ale or porter, produced from any quantity of malt, may be eafily afcertained; and thus the fair trader may be diftinguifhed from one who is fraudulent. The following example will fhew the good effect of ufing this inftrument. A certain

tain brewer who had compromifed matters with the excife-officers at the rate of one barrel and an half of fmall beer from the boll of malt, at which proportion only he was rated in the excife ledger, has ever fince paid, and is now paying, at the rate of four barrels and an half from the fame quantity ' By the new mode of furvey alfo, it was fuppofed to be in a manner impoffible that any fingle gauger, whatever his inclination might be, could fhew any great favour to the trader; for as the brewers now were not furveyed by one excifeman, or by more than one at the fame time of the day; all of them, coming in rotation, acted as checks upon one another. Hence it plainly appeared how grofsly the revenue had been defrauded in former times; as the amount of it, foon after the new method was adopted, rofe from L. 4691 · 15 . 8, to L. 10,817 · 12 : 9 *per annum*, being more than double what it had been, as already ftated.

FROM this great increafe of revenue, it was reafonable to conclude, that the Committee, if they did not ingratiate themfclves with the

Excife,

Excife, would at leaft have been allowed to carry on their bufinefs in peace; but fo far was this from being the cafe, that they found themfelves worfe than ever. The vengeance of the folicitor and furveyor-general was now thoroughly aroufed; and indeed it was not greatly to be wondered at; as the emoluments which, for fo long, had been put in their pockets, were now to be paid in to the public revenue. As it was not proper, however, to exprefs any difpleafure at this openly, Mr Maitland and his fupervifors, though they pretended to acquiefce in the new mode of furvey, made no exertions to enforce the full payment of duties, but became rather more lax in their furvey than before. Finding that nothing could be effected, while the whole body of Edinburgh brewers continued united, fome people have been wicked enough to al- ledge, that they began to practife with certain brewers, in order to detach them from their brethren, and perfuade them to act againft their common intereft. The temptation faid to be held out on this occafion, the only one indeed they had in their power to of- fer, was a promife, that fuch as relinquifhed

their

their adherence to the new plan, fhould find themfelves *no worfe than before*; and notwith-ftanding the experience the manufacturers already had of the mifchiefs arifing from fuch practices, fome were found weak enough to yield to this temptation. The confequences are eafy to be imagined: thefe who deferted the common caufe were treated with fuch lenity, that they got off for one-third of the legal duty, while the reft, who refufed to yield, were moft rigoroufly obliged to pay every penny that could be demanded; as will appear from an infpection of the mafh-ledger.

FROM this account of the matter, we can be at no lofs to difcover why the members of the Committee loft the favour of thefe falfe brethren. The excife-party, indeed, were foon fenfible of their own power; and had influence enough to call a meeting of the brewers, where, with unparalleled effrontery and inconfiftency, they voted the Committee, confifting of eleven members, ufelefs and nugatory, though they themfelves had appointed them, and they had proceeded exactly according to the directions of the whole body,

as will appear from the following agreement .———
ment .———

Edinburgh, Nov. 3. 1788.
AT a Meeting of the Committee of nine, appointed by a General Meeting of the Brewers in and about Edinburgh, on the 29th of October laſt,

PRESENT,
Mr JAMES EYRE, in the Chair.
Meſſ. John Cundell, Archibald Campbell, John Hunter, Archibald Campbell-Younger, Alexander Steven, George Gairdner, and Peter Hardie ; alſo preſent, Meſſ. David Cleghorn, John Hardie, Charles Cock, and James Anderſon, Brewers.

THE Committee having conſidered the reſolution of the general Meeting, and having taken under conſideration the preſent ſtate of the Brewers, report their opinion, That the only method to put them on an equal and reſpectful ſituation, will be by compelling every Brewer to pay the full Exciſe to Government, for the different kinds of Beer and Ale which ſhall be brewed and vended ;
and

and, in order to the carrying of this into execution, and for making frauds more easily
detected, That every Brewer should agree
not to mask sooner than six o'clock in the
morning, and the brewing, shall be finished,
the worts put into the coolers, and the length
declared at or before nine o'clock at night
That an agreement to the above purpose shall
be subscribed by such persons who shall be
present at the General Meeting, to be held
to-morrow, who chuse to do so, and to be
sent to those who may be absent, in order to
be signed by such who incline, and that a
Committee be appointed to apply to the Honourable the Commissioners of Excise, to take
the most effectual methods for preventing
of frauds, particularly with respect to those
who shall refuse to subscribe such agreement,
or who, having subscribed, shall fail to imple-
ment, or be guilty of any fraud; and the
Committee be authorised to wait upon the
Commissioners, and take such steps as may
appear most proper for keeping the Brewers
on an equal footing; and authorised the Pre-
ses to sign this report, and to deliver it to the
General Meeting.

(Signed) JAMES EYRE.

Edinburgh, Nov. 4. 1788.

AT a General Meeting of the Brewers this day, there were prefent, Meff. James Eyre, William Younger, Richard Younger, John Hardie, Archibald Campbell, Archibald Campbell-Younger, David Cleghorn, Peter Hardie, George Gairdner, David Kilgour, James Anderfon, Edward Home, Archibald Miln, Ifaac Salter, William Scott, Charles Salter, William Gordon, Thomas Laing, George Comb, John Craigie, Mathew Comb *jun.* William Ritchie, William Sinclair, Alexander Steven, William Giles, and Andrew Archer.

THE Meeting having read and confidered the above report of the Committee, approved thereof, and nominated and appointed the former Committee, along with Meff. David Cleghorn and John Hardie, any fix to be a quorum, as a Committee for carrying into execution the particulars mentioned in the foregoing report.—And we Subfcribers oblige us to regulate ourfelves agreeable thereto; the forefaid Committee being obliged to elect

three

three annually as members thereof, instead of three who are to go out—The above election of three to be made quarterly instead of annually.

Signed,

Mathew Comb.	Jas. Gordon.
Robert Barker.	Jas. Eyre.
Wm. Giles.	Geo. Gairdner.
Hugh Bell.	Alexr. Steven.
Wm. Gordon.	John Hardie.
Wm. Ritchie.	Wm. Younger.
Isaac Salter.	Richd. Younger.
Wm. Scott.	Archd. Campbell.
Archd. Milne.	Ar. Campbell-Younger.
Edw. Home.	John Craigie.
Jas. Anderson and Co.	David Cleghorn.
John Cundell.	Peter Hardie.
George Forest.	David Kilgour.
Alexr. Walker.	Mathew Comb, B.
John Notman.	John Hunter,
David Hodge.	Thos. Laing.
Janet Murray.	Andw. Archer.
Chas. Cock.	Chas. Salter.
Robt. Hamilton.	Geo. Comb.
Wilm. Manderson.	Willm. Sinclair.

SEVERAL

SEVERAL brewers particularly diftinguifhed themfelves on this occafion, by their oppo-
fition to the Committee which they themfelves
had appointed, that they might gain favour
with the Excife, and to accomplifh this purpofe,
were not afhamed to condemn the meafures
which they had formerly applauded. The
Committee being thus deferted, and confcious
that the only way by which they could extricate
themfelves was a vigorous exertion, determined to act for their own intereft, and for that of
the revenue, in the way they had originally
propofed. By procuring a fight of the excife
ledgers, they affured themfelves that matters
were as above reprefented; and the enormous
fraud thus committed on the revenue may
eafily be proved from an infpection of thefe
books. On the difcovery of this, and other
pieces of fcandalous behaviour on the part
of the furveyor-general, complaints were laid
before the Board of Excife, and applications
made for the removal of Mr Maitland from
the brewery department. The Board thought
proper to comply with the Committee's requeft:
Mr Maitland was removed, though ftill continued to furvey manufactures of greater im-

D   poitance

portance than the brewery, and Mr Burnet, a gentleman of honour and integrity, appointed in his stead. The following anecdote forms a striking contrast betwixt the behaviour of Mr Burnet and that of his predecessor —A short time after the appointment of the former, he was informed by Robert Laurie, one of Mr Maitland's most active supervisors, on the old plan of making discoveries at the expence of the revenue, that he suspected a certain brewer would abstract a great quantity of his worts, for which reason he proposed to make a survey next day, and thus the fraud would be discovered. This was entirely agreeable to the method in which Mr Maitland had all along proceeded; as the fine would have gone into the pockets of the excise-officers, and his friend the solicitor; but Mr Burnet, more attached to the faithful discharge of his duty, and to his oath of office, than to his private interest, told the surveyor, that if he suspected any such thing, he should instantly set an excise-man to watch, and to prevent any concealment from being made; adding, that he did not want frauds, but the security of the revenue, and that by

such

fuch a lax mode of furvey, L. 7000 a-year had been loft to the revenue, in the Edinburgh brewery alone.

AFTER the appointment of Mr Burnet to the office of furveyor-general, it was natural to fuppofe that the revenue would have been confiderably augmented; but inftead of this, no confiderable rife took place for three months. This unexpected circumftance fhewed, that the removal of Mr Maitland had not annihilated the influence of his party. Recourfe was therefore had a fecond time to the excife ledgers; from which, as well as from many concurrent teftimonies, it was found that the furveyors and other officers were ftill inactive in the performance of their duty; and it was even underftood that it would have been agreeable to Mr Maitland and his party to put an end to that reform which had been fo fucccfsfully begun by the Committee; and which could not be more effectually done than by reviving the lax mode of furvey, which had already proved fo detrimental to the revenue. Indeed, to fo great a length was this criminal laxity carried at the time we fpeak of, that from the books of excife

themfelves,

themfelves, it appears, that during the month of July 1789, the whole furveys of the four fupervifors, defigned as checks upon the inferior officers, amounted only to 22 days work of one man.

In confequence of this difcovery, an application was made to the Honourable Board for removing of the four fupervifors of Edinburgh diftrict, and requefting the appointment of three active and honeft men in quality of fupervifors; and this requeft was complied with by the Commiffioners, who were now fenfible that the propofals of the Committee had been attended with benefit to the revenue. The confequences now were fuch as equalled the moft fanguine expectations of thofe who had the good of the revenue at heart. Though the new fupervifors were appointed during the fummer feafon, when it is univerfally known that fermentation goes on more difadvantageoufly than at any other feafon, the monthly amount of the duties was augmented to almoft the higheft produce of the winter months in any preceding year; and, ever fince, the revenue has nearly tripled that

that of any preceding year during the continuance of the old fyſtem.

THE proceedings of the Committee continued to be highly diſagreeable to Mr Bonnar, who had now no other method left of accomplifhing his purpoſes, than by exerting his utmoſt efforts to have thoſe who favoured the reform treated with rigour, while thoſe who were not fhould be treated with equal lenity. Though the Committee had repeatedly mentioned to the Commiffioners, as well as addreffed the juſtices and folicitor by counſel, fetting forth that it was abſolutely neceffary to exact penalties proportionable to what appeared to be the degree of delinquency, with a view to prevent the commiffion of frauds, yet the old practice was ſtill continued. In many inſtances where the fraud was proved, the delinquents were very flightly fined, in others, inſtead of the full penalty, only $2\frac{1}{2}$ *per cent.* was exacted; thus plainly intimating, that for a very fmall fum His Majeſty's revenue might be defrauded to a very great amount, provided the delinquent was not a member of the Committee, or friendly to the fyſtem of reform

propoſed

propofed by it. With regard to the plan it-
felf, the folicitor has uniformly thrown upon
it all the abufe in his power As if it were not
poffible that the Edinburgh brewers fhould
ferioufly refolve to pay the duties, even when
they fee it for their intereft fo to do, he has
thought proper to fhew his wit, by ftigmati-
zing it with the names of the *Æra of Purity*,
or of the *Golden Age*, and the new mode of
furvey, which has been productive of fuch be-
neficial confequences, by the epithet of *the
courfing of a hare*. To his oratory muft we
likewife attribute that fhameful queftion generally put to brewers who have the misfortune to be called before the juftices, *viz.*
Whether they be of the reforming tribe? Is
there any effential difference between the de-
linquencies of a man who is a reformer, and
who is not? Is there not a fettled penalty in-
curred by every one who tranfgreffes the
laws by evading the duties? and dares any
man prefume to alter or evade that penalty, in
defiance of the determinations of the legiflature, while, at the fame time, he pretends to
adhere moft rigidly to the determinations of
the fame legiflature with regard to the eva-
fion.

fion of duties? The Committee infift for nothing but what the meaneft capacity muft in a moment determine to be fair and upright. They are willing to pay the full duties to government, and they afk no favour in any cafe for themfelves; but they infift, that whoever tranfgreffes the laws, fhall be fubjected to fuch penalties as may effectually prevent them from committing tranfgreffions of a fimilar kind in time to come. Thus only the trade can be put upon a fair and equal footing, the revenue increafed to its full proportion, and the public fupplied with goods of a proper quality. As long as individuals exercife fuch exorbitant difcretionary powers, it is impoffible that this can be the cafe. Judges indeed have a difcretionary power, to pronounce, or even mitigate, the fentence of the law, but they have no power to alter or reverfe its intention. As little have they to become parties, to delay caufes brought before them by people of a certain defcription, and to give exprefsly as a reafon, that they are *litigous*, and that the delay will procure the counfel another fee. Yet all this hath been done, and thofe who propofed the full

payment

payment of the duties have the mortification to perceive that all their labour is likely to be thrown away, and that almoſt entirely thro' the influence of a ſingle perſon. They have, however, the ſatisfaction of being conſcious that they have increaſed His Majeſty's revenue annually by a very conſiderable ſum, and that they have likewiſe pointed out a mode of ſurvey, which will for ever put it out of the power of the exciſe-men to connive at ſuch frauds as have formerly taken place ; and they ſtill hope the time is not diſtant when they may farther ſerve their country, by putting a ſtop, at leaſt in great part, to the importation of drink from England, which has been ſo long practiſed to the detriment of this kingdom. In the former method of ſurvey, when only one officer had the charge of a diviſion, it was always poſſible for that officer to connive at the frauds of the trader, by merely keeeping his books open till a proper opportunity offered of cloſing them to the mutual ſatisfaction of him and the trader ; but now the caſe is entirely altered. By the preſent method, the trader, though ſurveyed by an exciſe-man at one time of the day, is ſtill

liable

liable to another furvey the fame day by a different excife-man, and after that by a thiid, fourth, oi fifth. Should the firft of thefe grant any favour, at leaft one of any confequence, the fraud would certainly be detected by his brethren; and unlefs we can fuppofe fuch a number of excife-men to be in league with the traders, and with one another, there is an abfolute impoffibility of any fraud being committed. Should even this be the cafe, it would ftill be difficult; for now the books are not allowed to be kept open, but as foon as an excife-man has made his furvey, he is obliged to poft it into a ledger kept by the fupervifor, after which there can be no alteration. The Committee, howevei, tho'they cannot now receive any favour from the excife-officers, find that the latter, in conjunction with the folicitor, can bring them to a great deal of trouble. It may feem ftiange, that when a trader is confcious of integiity, and paying the duty on all occafions, he fhould have any reafon to fear an excife-man, or to be in danger fiom him. Nothing indeed of this kind could happen, if the excife-men were always willing to act uprightly, but the Com-

mittee

mitee complain that this is not the cafe; and
that their brethren are encouraged in their
iniquity by the folicitor, and even fupported
by the decifions of the juftices themfelves.
The advantage swhich the excife-men are now
enabled to take, arife from the extent of their
difcretionary powers, which are fo great, that
it is very difficult for an individual to fecure
himfelf againft their abufe, by any honefty or
fidelity on his part. An inftance of this a-
bufe has already been related, in the cafe of
a Member of the Committee. The excife-
man has a right to enter the works of every
brewer, at any time of the day or night; but
this does not imply that the doors fhall ftand
perpetually open, or that they fhall fly up at
the fight of an excife-man, as if opened by
divine power, or by magic. A few minutes
delay in this cafe is unavoidable from the nature of things; yet, in the prefent cafe, the
gate was not only broke down before it could
be opened with the key, but the proprietor
was fined in five pounds for not granting
admittance. This was an evident abufe of
this part of their difcretionary power, and to
prevent abufes of this kind, no other method

feems

feems practicable, but either to let the doors ftand open night and day, or to keep a watch-man on purpofe to admit the excife-officers when they take it into their heads to furvey.

ANOTHER piece of difcretionary power, which fome excife-officers feem now to claim, is, that of being perfectly deaf to the voice of truth, reafon, or common fenfe, when this deafnefs is capable of producing a fine, or bringing a manufacturer to trouble. It is faid by Mr Solicitor Bonnar to be againft the law for any brewer to make an in-creafe of his ftock without acquainting the excifeman, but there is no law which for-bids any part of the ftock which has once paid the duty from being carried out and re-turned back again without a fecond payment. For this, however, another member of the reform was brought into a very trouble-fome procefs, and fcarcely got off without a fine. The circumftance was as follows.—the brewer fent out two half hogfheads of ftrong ale to a cuftomer, which being reckoned defi-cient in quality, were returned. The excife-man charged thefe as an increafe of ftock; and, in defiance of every teftimony which

could

could be produced, dragged the proprietor into a procefs before the juftice of peace couit; from which, tho' he got off without a fine, he could not without much trouble and expence. A fimilar circumftance happened to the fame brewer on another occafion. It is part of the excife law, that worts, if furveyed while hot, fhall be allowed a tenth part for evaporation; but if the excife-man refufes to know whether they are hot or cold, he can thus at any time bring a manufacturer into a procefs, if not into a fine. This was alfo the cafe with the Committee brewer. A furvey had been made while the worts were very hot; another was made by one Corbet, a general furveyor, along with Laurie, the difcarded fupervifor from the brewery, before the worts were in a cold ftate; and at this fecond time the excife-men, in defiance of reafon and common fenfe, maintained that they were cold, when evidently hot; and as the full quantity had not yet gone off by evaporation, the proprietor was charged with a fraud; from which indeed he got off without a fine, but not without expence and trouble, as before. It is remarkable, that in this cafe, the brewer was put in the fraud fcheme, by

the

the furveyor-general Corbet, though two fupervifors depofed that the worts weie actually
hot at the time the furvey was made.

OTHER inftances are, if poffible, ftill more
glaring and intolerable. An excife-man, in
furveying the work of another brewer,
made a miftake of two barrels, and though
repeatedly told by the fervant that he was
miftaken, refufed to be convinced. Next
morning, however, he increafed the two barrels he had omitted in the evening, charged
the proprietor with a fraudulent increafe of
ftock, and involved him in a procefs; telling
the fervant that, " his word would be taken
" before his" (the fervant's). As the brewer
was known to have been active in the affair
of reform, the procefs was fo agreeable to
Bonnar, that the excife-man thought proper
to repeat his experiment on a larger fcale; and
therefore, at another furvey, made a miftake
of *eighteen* barrels, which in like manner were
difcovered. Scandalous and barefaced as this
was, it would probably have brought on a
fecond procefs, had not another officer luck-
ily been attending the works all the time be-

twixt

twixt the two furveys; fo that the treacherous intention of the former was detected. On reprefenting this cafe to the Board, the excife-man was broke; but notwithftanding his delinquency, Bonnar thought proper to profecute the brewer a fecond time for the former fuppofed offence, infifting, in the open court, that the word of an excife-officer ought rather to be believed than that of any evidence whatever.

In a third inftance, in which the above brewer was concerned, he did not come off fo eafily. An excife-man, attending the running off a copper of $19\frac{1}{2}$ barrels worts, afked the fervant concerning its length, or the quantity of worts of different kinds it would produce. To fuch queftions the brewer cannot give an anfwer, till the operation be finifhed, though he is obliged to anfwer " before any part of the guile is cleanfed out of his tuns, or other veffels or utenfils." In the prefent inftance, the fervant anfwered, that he could not then tell the length, as the operation was not finifhed, but that he would do fo next morning, when the whole worts would be run off. The excife-man afked no more queftions,

tions, but inserted the whole in his book as a
fraud, for which the brewer, contrary to law,
was condemned in the full penalty of L. 19 10s.
But granting that the fraud was real, which
all parties agreed was not the case, why is
this brewer condemned in the full penalty,
when others in a worse predicament are allowed to pass for nothing, or for the most trifling
sum? The case of Mrs Anderson brewer in
Leith is still more glaring she was fined in
one court to near the amount of L. 60 Sterling,
without being guilty of any trespass but one,
the full penalty of which was L 7 10s.—In one
instance, a vessel, standing in an entered cellar,
was construed into a concealment, for which
she was fined L. 12 10s. Sterling. Unluckily
for any trader who falls under such sentences,
there is no appeal to a higher tribunal. From
actual transgressions of the same nature, these
brewers who were not in the Committee were
acquitted, which established the report, that different decisions were given to different persons,
as best suited the mysterious designs of the
solicitor of excise, &c.

It is this open and scandalous partiality
which now constitutes the principle grievance

of thofe brewers who are willing at all times
to pay the whole duties, and which they are
now convinced will contribute to the advancement of their own intereft, as well as to the
increafe of the revenue. For this purpofe,
they have, as individuals, fubjected themfeves
to a very confiderable rifk. They have, in
the firft place, to contend with all their brethren who are difaffected to the caufe, and
who are ftill fo infatuated as not to fee that
their true intereft lies in a perfect compliance
with the laws, and not in a conftant attempt
to evade them. To brewers of this defcription, the new mode of furvey muft be highly
difagreeable, as allowing no room for fraud
on their part, nor favour on that of the excife-
men, unlefs the latter were fupported by the
folicitor. But were their wifhes to be accomplifhed, the Members of the Committee muft
find themfelves in the greateft danger of being
utterly ruined. Were the old mode of furvey to be adopted, it would then be in the
power of any excife-man, in conjunction
with the folicitor, to grant what favours he
pleafed to an individual, as formerly practifed; thus putting it in his power to underfell

his

his neighbours, though at the expence of the quality of his drink. The Members of the Committee, and all others friendly to their cause, who have no favour to expect, muſt of course be obliged either to give up buſineſs altogether, or attempt, at the greateſt riſk, to evade the duties payable to government, or to make their liquor of a bad quality, as has already been obſerved, to the detriment of the public at large, as well as of the revenue. But beſides this *unequal* conteſt, they have, in the next place, to engage with almoſt all the excise-officers themſelves, whoſe intereſt it is to connive with the brewers in the manner already mentioned; as, by having a ſhare in the fines, they would thus become poſſeſſed of many perquiſites which they cannot by any means obtain at preſent, nor while the new mode of ſurvey is continued. It may be ſaid, indeed, if the ſmuggling brewers are fined, how is it to be ſuppoſed that they will carry on a trade evidently to their own prejudice? But the anſwer to this is obvious;—a brewer can afford to allow the detection of one barrel, and to be fined in a ſmall ſum for it, provided he is allowed to carry off hun-

E   dreds

dreds without detection. neither can the small-
nefs of the fines be any objection to what is
juft now advanced ; as the number makes up
for the deficiency in this refpect ; and the
whole lofs devolves ultimately upon the revenue, and fuch brewers as pay the full duties. The great lofs formerly fuftained by
the revenue is moft evident from an infpection of the excife books, before and after the
new mode of furvey took place. The very
firft month after the application was made,
even before the new method took place, fo
great was the alarm among the gaugers on
account of the propofal, that by merely exerting themfelves, and doing their duty better
than formerly, the revenue was augmented
by no lefs than 236 pounds. The next
month there was an encreafe of 40 pounds a-
bove the former ; and the third month of
118 pounds. From that time the rife has
been fo amazing, that it is impoffible for
any perfon to believe that the former defi-
ciency could be occafioned by any thing elfe
than a remiffnefs, or rather wilful negligence
of the excife-men, in conjunction with the
brewers. Thus, in January 1788, the a-
mount

mount of the revenue was L.457 14 3; in January 1790 it was L.987 10 10, in February 1788 it amounted to L.420.19:9; the fame month of 1790, it was no lefs than L.1038.1 3. A proportional increafe has been found in every fucceeding month thus in March 1788 the whole amount was no more than L.387 18.7, while in March 1790 it was L.902 6s.; In April 1788 it was L.416 19 10; but in April 1790 the fum was augmented to L.1140.7 3 Yet all this time, when the revenue was fo deficient, the fines of brewers were very frequent, and the excife-officers appeared to be exceedingly active in detecting the fraudulent practices of thofe whom they furveyed. The matter then is evident to demonftration, that however this mode of furvey and inflicting arbitrary fines may anfwer the purpofes of the excife-men, or of particular brewers, it anfwers none to government, and confequently that it ought to have been laid afide, and no thoughts of renewing it ever entertained.

BUT befides the body of inferior officers, the brewers who ftand forth for the reform-

ed

ed method of furvey have to bear the weight of Mr Bonnar's refentment, the prefent folicitor of excife, in which indeed the new furveyor-general feems to be involved no lefs than they. The reafon of Mr Bonnar's difpleafure is very evident; namely, that he is entitled to a very confiderable fhare of the fines, infomuch, that his office was fuppofed to be worth no lefs than L. 1800 *per annum*, when both brewery and diftillery were under the excife. No wonder then, that now when fuch a confiderable decreafe of his revenue, *viz.* no lefs than four hundred pounds Sterling, is likely to take place, he fhould vent his wrath in every poffible manner. A moft glaring inftance of this, was his caufing Mr Hope, the king's counfel, charge the Committee in open court with a diabolical fcheme*, invented and calculated to deftroy the fmall brewers; while in fact the fcheme, as he called it, was ultimately for the intereft of the fmall brewers, as well as thofe who could afford to carry on their operations on a larger fcale; the reafon of

---

* *Query.* Does a plan that is calculated to fecure the revenue, and to prevent partiality in the execution of the laws, deferve the epithet of DIABOLICAL?

of which has been already explained. How
far it is proper, that a folicitor of excife
fhould be admitted to any fhare in the fines
arifing from frauds on the revenue, is fub-
mitted to the judgment of the public. certain
it is, that in England no fuch cuftom pre-
vails, and it is equally certain, that the allowing a folicitor, or any perfon elfe, to have a
fhare in fines, muft be a temptation to him
to wifh for an increafe of their number, and
to deviate from that ftrict impartiality which
it is the duty of every one in public office to
obferve, efpecially of one whofe official fituation gives him great influence over the
Board of Excife. In many inftances, however, it is evident that Mr Bonnar, inftead of
being impartial, has violated every rule of de-
cency towards his fuperiors, when he found
that his own partiality and refentment could
not be adopted againft thofe who had offended him by *paying their full duties to government.*
Thus, in one of the caufes againft a brewer before mentioned, Mr Bonnar thought
proper to reflect upon the Honourable Commiffioners themfelves, faying, in open court,
that they had acted wrong, and he would

tell

tell them fo, as if they had been incapable of performing their duty, or had not known how to execute it. We are forry thus to make fuch a public attack on an individual; but when an individual is entrufted with any office by the king, and in confequence of that office enjoys the public confidence, if he abufes that confidence by fuch fcandalous partiality as Mr Bonnar can be proved to have exercifed, we may furely fay that he betrays the king, forfeits all title to the regard of his countrymen, and that his conduct cannot be too feverely animadverted upon.

How much the refentment not only of Mr Bonnar, but of the reft of that party was excited by the adoption of the new mode of furvey, and the confequent increafe of revenue, is evident from the following facts. The city of Edinburgh draws a duty of one fixth of a penny upon every Scots pint of ale, which duty is exacted agreeable to the quantity charged by the excife-officer; and which, under the new furveyor Mr Burnet, and the fupervifors fubordinate to him, has been
augmented

augmented to a very confiderable fum. On this account, in the month of February 1790, the town council of Edinburgh, with confent of the Commiffioners of Excife, ordered fixty guineas to be paid to Mr Burnet, and twenty to each of the three fupervifors under him, as a teftimony of the fenfe they had of the fidelity and integrity with which thefe officers had difcharged their duty Mr Maitland, the former furveyor, complained of this gift, by letters addreffed to each of the five Commiffioners, as being a tacit reflection on his conduct, as he pretended that the amounts were as high from January 5. to July 5. 1789, when the brewery was under his management, as they were in the fix months from July 5. to the 5th of January laft, when Mr Burnet had the management of it. This ftate of the matter, however, was evidently unfair ; as during the former period, there is always a greater quantity of drink brewed than during the latter, which will eafily be feen from the ftatement of the revenue already given for fome time paft. Nothing indeed can be more plain, than that a vaft increafe of revenue has taken place fince the

new

new method of furvey was adopted, and Mr
Burnet appointed to the office of furveyor-general. To the proofs which have already
been offered on this fubject, we fhall only add
the following comparifon, *viz.* that the a-
mount of the duties for four months, ending
with the 5th of April 1790, is L.4017.9.11,
while, during the fame period in 1788, it was
no more than L.1719·6:4; the balance in
favour of the new mode of furvey being no
lefs than L.2298:3.7, in that fhort fpace of
time. Obfervations of the fame kind, but e-
qually prepofterous and ill founded with
thofe of Mr Maitland, were made by the King's
counfel, at the defire of Mr Bonnar himfelf,
who attempted to prove, from the ftatement
already given, that there was a rife in the revenue during the time that Mr Maitland of-
ficiated. The fallacy of his affertions, however, are obvious from the very authority to
which he appealed; which, though it has already been repeatedly taken notice of, we
fhall once more fet forth in its proper point
of view. In the month of April 1788, the a-
mount of the revenue was L.416.19·10; in
May, the fame year, L.394:13.6; in June,
L.382

L 382 19 9; in July, L.334. 10. 2, in Au-
guſt, L.316. 7. 5; in September, L.333 7: 6;
in October, L.334 : 3. 8. It is impoſſible that
any perſon can, with the leaſt appearance of
truth, ſay, that there was any riſe of the revenue during theſe ſix months : on the contrary, there was an evident decreaſe from
L.416 to L.334; not indeed abſolutely without intermiſſion, for then in a ſhort time there
muſt have been no revenue at all; but ſuch
as ſhewed that government was ſome how or
other defrauded of its right; and that the
exciſe-officers were either unable or unwill-
ing to counteract theſe frauds. That it was
neglect of duty, and not inability in the exciſe-officers, which had the occaſion of this, is
likewiſe evident from the great riſe which
inſtantly took place, on the application being
made to the Commiſſioners for a new mode
of ſurvey. Thus, in the month of November, on the 6th day of which the application
was made, the revenue was increaſed by
L.103 14 1, and the following month by
L.339 : 7. 3, more than it had been in October. How came it to paſs that ſuch a ſudden
riſe ſhould take place in theſe two months, and
that

that the revenue fhould be doubled in fuch a fhort time? No fuch thing had happened the preceding year; for in the month of November 1787 the revenue was only L 416 : 7 8; and in the month of December, no more than L.423 12 : 7. Shall we fuppofe that the brewers in Edinburgh had in the month of October 1788 refolved to brew twice the quantity of liquor which fufficed their cuftomers? or fhail we fuppofe, that in the month of November that year, the inhabitants of the metropolis were vifited by a raging thirft, which has continued to increafe ever fince? Is it not evident, that previous to the application for a new mode of furvey, the whole poffe of excife-officers had been neglecting their duty, and fuffering the brewers to defraud the revenue, on purpofe that they might fill the pockets of the folicitor, &c. with the fines which would frequently arife from detections, tho' thefe detections bore but a fmall proportion to the quantity which was fmuggled, to the great detriment of the revenue? On the other hand, is it not now equally evident, from the great augmentation of revenue, that few or no frauds are committed of near-

ly

ly equal magnitude with the former, and that the excife-men are doing their duty much better? Is it not equally evident alfo, that the exceffive difpleafure of the folicitor, and the perfecution commenced againft Mr Burnet the prefent furveyor-general, cannot be the effect of zeal for the revenue, but of the refent-ment of fome intereſted people, on account of a diminution of their profits by the full payment of the duties. At his defire, it has been furmifed, an inquiry was made into the conduct of Mr Burnet and his offi-cers, without any juft pretence of defi-ciency of revenue, the only thing that could render fuch a ftep neceffary *. A Mr Corbet, one of the general fupervifors refiding at Stirling, was pitched upon for the purpofe; and in what manner he conducted the inquiry will beft appear from the follow-ing facts. On his commencement, he expref-

fed

---

* Would it not have been more confiftent with the duty of Mr Bonner, to have caufed an enquiry to be made into the conduct of Mr Maitland, the predeceffor of Mr Burnet Under Maitland's management, the brewery revenue had dwindled down to a perfect trifle—under Mr Burnet it has been nearly tripled *Ob t infra a' O i oi cs'*

fed the greateſt enmity to thoſe traders who had promoted the new mode of ſurvey; proceeding even ſo far as to ſay, that could he find them out in any fault, it would give him the greateſt pleaſure. It can be proved alſo that he made uſe of threats to intimidate the officers; telling Mr Millar ſurveyor in the Canongate, that he himſelf, with Mr Leven, were to ſurvey as generals upon the brewers; that Mr Millar would ſoon have no occaſion for the ſtools in his exciſe-chamber, intimating thereby, that he and the preſent ſet of ſupervifors were to be turned off. On aſking Mr Hannah, ſupervifor at Leith, about the conduct of Mr Burnet, and not receiving ſuch anſwers as he wiſhed, he proceeded to execrate Mr Hannah, and to tell him, that he could give other information if he had a mind. In the very taking of the depoſitions of the witneſſes who were examined, the ſame partiality was obſerved. Previous to the examination, the witneſſes were aſked what they had to ſay; and on not receiving ſuch anſwers as he defired, the ſame mode of execration was followed, with a threat to turn the exciſe-men out of their

place,

places, if they did not take care. In some
cafes the depofitions were not allowed to be
taken down; and, in fhort, it was evident that
he wifhed none to be examined but thofe
who were ill affected to the officers employed
at that time; and there is great reafon to believe, that thefe perfons were pointed out by
fome who were interefted in the abolition of
the new mode of furvey, and re-eftablifhment
of the old. That this was really the cafe, becomes ftill more probable, when it is confidered, that on Mr Corbet's giving in a report to
the Commiffioners of Mr Burnet's conduct,
he ftuffed the paper with fuch falfehoods as,
had they operated according to his wifh,
would certainly have turned Mr Burnet out of
his place. He has however been allowed, contrary to the ufual cuftom in fuch cafes, to
anfwer his report; a degree of indulgence
which certainly fhows that the Commiffioners
were fenfible of his having done his duty;
and the great length of time during which
this matter has been depending, plainly evin-
ces the difficulty which Mr Corbet has to
fubftantiate his charges; as well as that the
Com-

Commissioners are determined to investigate
the affair in the most complete manner.

We shall close the disagreeable task of making animadversions on the conduct of individuals, with one other anecdote relative to
the gentleman last mentioned, and the reason of giving this anecdote is, that it leads
to the decision of a point most important in
its nature to the revenue, to the public in
general, and to the brewers as individuals.
While the depositions regarding Mr Burnet's
conduct were taking down, Mr Corbet, with
a view no doubt of showing his own dili-
gence and activity in business, thought proper to inform the bystanders. that at a court
lately held at Dunfermline, no less than
20,000 gallons of ale concealments were
brought to light. This speech plainly show-
ed that his ideas were entirely perverted, so
that he really did not know the duty of his
office. It is certainly obvious to every one
who bestows a moment's consideration upon
the subject, that the intention of the legisla-
ture in making excise laws, and appointing
excise-officers to collect the duties, is not to
obtain

obtain fines by allowing thefe laws to be e-
vaded, but to obtain a revenue for the purpofes of government. The anfwer made by
Mr Burnet to this innuendo of Mr Corbet
was exceedingly proper, *viz.* that if he (Mr
Corbet) and his officers had done their duty,
by fecuring the revnue, in the firft inftance,
there would have been no concealments to be
found. It is the duty of an excife-man not
to *detect frauds*, but to *prevent* them from being committed. The former indeed is of advantage to the excife-man, becaufe he receives
part of the fine, but the latter is only of advantage to the revenue; becaufe the number
of detections bear but a fmall proportion to
that of the frauds which efcape with impunity. Hence Mr Burnet very juftly obferved,
that had Mr Corbet and his officers done
their duty in the manner above mentioned,
it would have put no money in their pockets.
Nothing can be more eafy, than for the exc fe-
officers to prevent frauds, though it may not
be always in their power to detect them.
They have only to appoint one to watch the
operation of brewing, and the brewer is obliged to admit of their attendance as long as

they pleafe. Thus, if they think proper, it is altogether impoffible for the brewer to fmuggle any quantity, great or fmall, without the connivance of the excife-man; and by the new method of furvey, it is impoffible for an excife-man to connive as formerly with a fraudulent brewer. Why then fhould Mr Bonnar, or any other perfon, who pretends to act for the intereft of the excife, find fault with a mode of furvey which abfolutely prevents a poffibility of fraud in either party? or why fhould profecutions be raifed againft thofe excife-officers who have manifefted an attention to their duty, by augmenting the revenue to more than double of what it formerly was. Ought not rather profecutions to be raifed againft thofe under whofe management the revenue was loft, and inquiries made into their conduct, in order to prevent the commiffion of fimilar frauds in time to come. The prefent excife-officers have not, it is true, detected as many frauds as formerly; but the reafon of this is obvious, *viz.* that by the faithful difcharge of their duty, there are not now fo many frauds to be detected. This may be, nay, it certainly is, a very ma-

nive

terial difadvantage to all thofe who receive any emolument from the fines inflicted upon fraudulent traders, but by the increafe of revenue, government would eafily be able to make fuch an additional augmentation to their falary, as would put them beyond the reach of any temptation to encourage, or connive at any of thofe mean fraudulent fchemes which both parties were formerly in a manner obliged to follow; the brewers to keep their credit, and the excife-men to procure themfelves a decent fubfiftence.

On the whole, it is not wifhed, by any means, to fet forth an individual, or any number of individuals, as objects of the public refentment, or their office as unworthy of having an exiftence. The attention of the public is requefted to what is really their own intereft, *viz.* To take the proper means for procuring malt liquors of the beft quality, and which never can be done while the trade of fmuggling goes on. It has generally been imagined, that the duties upon malt liquors are too high to be fully paid with any profit

F   to

to the trader; but this is undoubtedly a miſtake. It is abſurd to ſuppoſe that government would lay on a tax upon malt liquors which could not be paid, and it is equally abſurd to imagine that the Edinburgh brewers would join in a petition to enforce the full payment of duties which they knew muſt end in their own ruin. The event has already diſproved the notion: the revenue has been almoſt tripled, and the brewers are not in worſe circumſtances than before. By having time to conduct their operations properly, and without hurry or fear, the brewers can now draw off ſo much more liquor, that the lengths they now run are capable of enabling them to pay their preſent large duty, better than all the ſmuggling they formerly practiſed could enable them to pay their ſmall one. Thus alſo the quality of the liquors muſt be greatly improved, and the vaſt importation from England, which has long been continually increaſing, will, it is to be hoped, be at laſt diminiſhed, and much money kept in the country which has been exported. To accompliſh theſe deſireable purpoſes, purpofes, the brewers have nothing to afk farther, than that the mode of furvey, which has been for fome time adopted in Edinburgh, be extended throughout Scotland, that no undue preference may be fhown, but that the whole trade may be put on an equality. Application has been already made by the brewers for this purpofe; but they have had the mortification to find themfelves unable to procure an extenfion of it even as far as Dalkeith. The attention of the public in general, particularly of the landed gentlemen, whofe intereft it effentially concerns, is therefore requefted, in order to accomplifh a point for which the late applications have been found ineffectual.

THE manufacturing of malt liquor in this country has always been inferior to that of England. One great caufe of this inferiority arifes undoubtedly from the baneful method, connived at by excife-men, in which the bufinefs was formerly carried on. Thus, though a brewer might do tolerably well while he carried on his works on a fmall

fcale,

scale, yet the moment he began to enlarge them, he found himself in a quite different situation. The reason was evident, *viz.* that whatever indulgence the excise-men might be inclined to grant him on the former scale, it was found impossible to do so in an equal proportion when the works were enlarged. Hence, all attempts to enlarge the breweries of Scotland have uniformly failed, and ended in the ruin of those who made the attempt. In England the case is far otherwise. In Newcastle, York, and even in all the small towns of that kingdom, the brewery is carried on upon a most extensive plan, and the liquors are produced of a quality very much superior to any which this country can boast of. If ever Scotland is to be set upon an equality with the sister kingdom in the manufacture of malt liquors, it can only be done by regulating the collection of the duty in such a manner, that neither brewers nor excise-men can have it in their power to behave in a fraudulent manner From neglecting this, the revenue has been diminished, the quality of the liquor spoiled, and the

trade

trade almoſt entirely ruined. By extending over the kingdom ſuch a mode of ſurvey as has been adopted in Edinburgh, matters may in ſome time undoubtedly be remedied; but without ſuch an extenſion, it is to be feared that the ſmugglers, in conjunction with corrupt officers of exciſe, &c. may ſtill be able effectually to overthrow the fair traders, and render it impoſſible for them either to manufacture liquors of a good quality, or even to carry on their buſineſs with advantage to themſelves or to their country.

F I N I S.

CPSIA information can be obtained at www.ICGtesting.com
Printed in the USA
LVOW112248250113

317257LV00004B/219/P